Leptin Resistan

Start Using the Ultimate Fat Burning Hormone Leptin To Lose Weight Naturally while Promoting Good Health

Table Of Contents

Introduction

I want to thank you and congratulate you for downloading the book *Leptin Resistance: Start Using the Ultimate Fat Burning Hormone Leptin To Lose Weight Naturally while Promoting Good Health.*

This book contains proven steps and strategies on how to control leptin levels and improve the body's sensitivity to leptin. Recent studies have shown a strong link between obesity and leptin. This hormone has even been dubbed as the single hormone that directly affects weight gain. Numerous studies have shown just how much leptin influences the body's functioning in terms of regulating hunger, eating, and fat storage patterns.

Here's an inescapable fact: you will need to understand just how the body controls its many functions. It has a carefully orchestrated homeostatic process that keeps everything within the narrow normal range. It may even be surprising to know that the body has an inherent mechanism to prevent excessive eating and weight gain. It is able to control certain factors in order to preserve itself- to protect from starving and from eating too much. However effective this mechanism is, certain factors can cause an imbalance. It may surprise you to know that small and seemingly innocent daily actions and choices can disrupt the careful balance in the body. Imbalances predispose the body to develop several chronic conditions.

If you do not develop your leptin sensitivity and normal control mechanism, the body will be at a higher risk of more serious and even life threatening conditions. Leptin may only seem like an insignificant hormone, but causing it to get out of balance can trigger a cascade of health problems.

It's time for you to find out and understand just what leptin and leptin resistance are, how it happens, and what you can do to prevent and reverse it. The solutions are pretty simple once true understanding is gained. Read this book to change your health and turn your life around today.

Chapter 1: The Hormone Leptin

Numerous hormones in the body influence every metabolic process. One of these hormones is leptin. In recent years, this protein hormone has been gaining more attention because of its association with weight control. The hormone leptin has a role in regulating the energy intake and expenditure of the body, particularly in food intake, appetite, and metabolism.

What is Leptin?

Fat tissues in the body produce the hormone leptin. The name is derived from the Greek word *leptos*, meaning thin—an apt term for a hormone that directly influences weight. When kept at the right levels, leptin has a potential to cause weight loss.

Levels of leptin in the body depend on how many fat cells are producing it. So basically, more leptin means more fat cells.

Leptin is an adipose-derived protein hormone. It is produced by the white fatty deposits in the body. The amount of leptin in the body roughly indicates the total amounts of fats. That is, more leptin means more fats in the body are producing it. Less leptin means less white fat deposits that produce it.

Aside from white fat deposits, brown fats also produce leptin in very small amounts. This hormone is also produced in minute amounts by other body organs such as the skeletal muscles, bone marrow, fundic glands (found in the stomach), ovaries, liver, placenta, and the pituitary gland.

Function of Leptin

The main functions of leptin include the following:

- Controlling the body's metabolic rate
- Regulating hunger sensations
- Controlling energy consumption

Leptin also influences the brain in terms of the following:

- Brain structure and overall functioning
- Mental focus and sharpness
- Memory enhancement
- Mood enhancement

When the body's fat cells release leptin, it signals the brain that there is enough stored energy. The brain then sends signals to other parts of the body, reducing hunger sensations. This natural process prevents one from overeating.

A surge in leptin tells the brain that is there enough fat stores and there is no need to eat more and no immediate need to store fat. At certain levels, leptin may also signal the body to start burning excess fat. If leptin levels are low, the brain recognizes it as starvation. It means that there are too few fat cells that produce leptin. It stimulates the body to start preserving fats, preventing fat burning. The brain slows down metabolism and increases appetite. All of these aim to induce more calorie intake for more fat conversion and storage.

Leptin is also a primary hormone that controls hunger. More leptin means more fats, so the body does not need to eat. It signals the brain to stop feeling hungry because there is no need for nourishment. Leptin also slows down the production and release of other hormones that promote appetite. It also promotes the release of another appetite-suppressing hormone, ghrelin.

In the hypothalamus, leptin counteracts the effects of a compound called neuropeptide Y which is a potent compound that promotes hunger. Neuropeptide Y is secreted by both the hypothalamus and the gut cells. The amount of neuropeptide Y secreted by the gut cells is considerably lower than the hypothalamus. Smaller amounts mean less potent effects on the body.

Leptin also counteracts the effects of another compound called anandamide. This is also a hunger-promoting compound that binds to receptors similar to THC (tetrahydrocannabinol) receptors.

Aside from inhibiting hunger-promoting compounds, leptin also influences the synthesis of a hunger-suppressing compound called α-MSH.

Appetite suppression brought about by leptin lasts longer than ones caused by other appetite-suppressing compounds in the body. Uncontrolled hunger results from low levels of leptin or from cellular resistance to leptin.

Leptin Levels

Hormonal levels fluctuate throughout the day. For leptin, the highest levels are normally between midnight and the early hours of the morning. Experts believe that high leptin levels during this period are the explanation for one not going hungry at night. Leptin fluctuations occur during the "active" hours of the day and largely depend on the meal times. A person who is used to eating at certain times of the day will expect leptin levels to correspond to the regular scheduled meal times. For example, a person used to eating at 8 in the morning will expect leptin levels to be low around this time.

Leptin levels also react to certain body activities and conditions such as the following:

- Short term fasting, usually around 24 to 72 hours, can lead to decreased leptin levels, even if there are no significant changes in the fat mass.

- Starvation causes leptin levels to decrease as an adaptive and self-reservation response.

- Sleep influences leptin levels.

  Studies have found out that restful, unbroken sleep of 8 to 12 hours every night brings leptin levels up to normal. Sleep deprivation has been linked to higher leptin levels.

  Obese people who suffer from obstructive sleep apnea have been found to have increased leptin levels. The levels decrease when CPAP (continuous positive airway pressure) is administered.

- Emotional stress is linked to increased leptin levels.

- Increased testosterone levels decrease leptin levels.

- Increased estrogen levels increase leptin levels in the body.

- Leptin levels are decreased after long term physical exercise and training.

- Leptin levels increase in the presence of insulin.

- Dexamethasone increases the levels of leptin.

- Obesity increases the levels of leptin, paradoxically.

High levels of leptin in the body promote inflammation. This condition also puts the body at higher risk of chronic conditions such as diabetes, heart diseases, and arthritis among others.

High levels can contribute to the following symptoms:

- High blood pressure

- Insulin resistance

- Heart disease

How is Leptin Level Controlled?

The main organ that controls leptin levels is the brain, particularly the hypothalamus. There are numerous leptin receptors on the hypothalamic cells, which are very sensitive to the level of leptin in the blood. High levels of leptin in the blood stimulate the receptors in the hypothalamus. The brain then sends a signal to the rest of the body, indicating that there is enough fuel for the body to use. This signal is interpreted as feeling full. In response to this signal, the body increases its metabolic rate. When the levels of leptin decrease, the brain interprets this as declining fuel levels for metabolic processes. The brain produces a hunger signal. The body reduces its metabolic rate and feels hungry. Aside from the hypothalamus, other tissues in the body also have leptin receptors on their surfaces. These receptors respond to leptin levels and also play certain roles in the overall appetite and weight regulation.

Calorie deficits lower leptin levels. It also stimulates the metabolic rate to slow down. The slower the metabolism gets, the harder it is to burn fats. This is a normal body response to prevent the body from consuming all the fats. When all fats in the body are burned, the organs lose very important cushions and insulations, making the body more prone to damage from all sorts of factors. The body will also start to digest proteins from muscles- a very dangerous condition to be in. Hence, declining leptin levels makes fat burning more difficult.

On the other hand, chronic high levels of leptin can be very dangerous. High leptin levels mean higher metabolic rates. This poses a threat to the body. High metabolic rates mean increased body temperatures and accelerated chemical processes. The body will start to feel threatened with a long-term high metabolic rate. It will eventually send signals to other organs and tissues to ignore the high levels of leptin in order to decrease metabolism. This will bring about leptin resistance. Once the body becomes leptin resistant, the body tends to hoard more fat rather than stay lean.

How to keep leptin levels within normal limits?

Staying lean is the best way to prevent leptin resistance. Weight gain is linked to leptin resistance because the excess fats block leptin function and signal. Excess weight also tends to cause hormonal imbalance—not just for leptin, but other hormones as well.

Aim to balance macronutrient intake. Having too little carbohydrate intake can also reduce metabolism because the body recognizes inadequate carbohydrate intake as starvation. Starvation will throw off normal leptin levels in the body. When following a low-carbohydrate diet, aim to have a cheat or refeed day. This means allowing the body to get a carbohydrate jolt once in a while.

Chapter 2: Leptin Resistance

Leptin resistance occurs when the body may be producing a lot of leptin, but the appetite suppression effect does not kick in. This is mainly because the cellular receptors do not recognize the leptin signal.

When leptin resistance happens, the brain is not sensitive to the amounts of leptin brought by the blood. Hence, it has a false notion that the body does not have enough stored energy. It sends a signal, a desire to eat more. The net result is weight gain. Because of this cycle, leptin resistance is now being closely studied as a probable cause for obesity. The body loses its natural check and balance, causing the person to eat beyond what the body needs (overeating), resulting in excessive weight gain or obesity.

Studies have shown that it is more about leptin resistance rather than low amounts of leptin that contributes to obesity and weight loss difficulties. The resistance, or the inability to recognize the signal given by leptin, puts the body under a false sense of starvation. In response to the perceived starvation, the body sets off a multitude of metabolic reactions that intend to increase the body's fat stores. It also thwarts any attempt by the body to burn fat and to lose weight. The body actually enters a fat/energy preservation mode; so any attempt to burn stored fat is doubly counteracted by the body.

Also, leptin resistance affects the action of the thyroid hormones. These hormones are among the primary hormones that regulate the rate of metabolism. The more thyroid hormones are in the body, the faster the rate of metabolism. In leptin resistance, reverse T3 is formed instead of the normal thyroid hormones. This reverse T3 blocks the normal effects of thyroid hormone in the body, contributing to weight gain.

How leptin resistance occurs

In simple terms, leptin resistance develops similar to how insulin resistance develops. The body cells become less sensitive due to chronic overexposure to leptin. Long-term, continuous exposure to high leptin levels causes the cells to shut themselves down to prevent fatigue and damage.

One factor that can trigger surge in leptin levels is eating food high in sugar, particularly fructose. The fat cells are the main cells that metabolize fructose. More fructose means more fat cell activity and more leptin released.

Causes of Leptin Resistance

There is no single factor that leads directly to leptin resistance. It is more of a combination of several factors that set the stage for this condition to occur.

Fructose

This is the single most important compound that contributes largely to the development of leptin resistance. Studies found that fructose, especially HFCS (high fructose corn syrup), blocks the body's appetite control mechanism, impedes fat burning, and stimulates fat building in the liver.

The chemical structure of fructose has the ability to mess up with the body's appetite and hunger control mechanisms. It makes the leptin receptors on the cells less responsive to the hormone. It blocks the body from realizing it is already full. If a person does not feel full and satiated, overeating happens.

Fructose also has been linked to poor fat burning. It actually delays or hinders the body from burning the stored fat. So, overeating plus slow fat burning is definitely a go for obesity. As this condition progresses, the body tissues, especially the brain, becomes resistant to any level of leptin that may show up in the blood.

A study has also shown that fructose in food reduces the effect of a low-carb diet. The liver is designed to convert carbohydrates into fat for storage. More carbohydrates mean faster conversion into fat that are stored in the liver and in other body tissues. A low carbohydrate diet aims to provide very little materials for the liver to turn into fat. Low carbohydrates available in the body mean less fat produced by the liver. However, if going low-carb but the food is high on fructose, fat production by the liver continues. Fructose actually stimulates the liver to continue converting other macronutrients and calories (i.e., proteins) into fat.

Carbohydrates

Carbohydrate is an essential macronutrient that the body needs for a wide range of purposes. However, not all carbohydrates are created equal. There are good carbohydrates, but there are also "bad" ones. Good carbohydrates provide the body with the energy it needs for various chemical and metabolic processes. Bad carbohydrates set off a cycle that messes up the homeostasis. One particular type of bad carbohydrate is refined or white carbohydrates. This is found in refined white flour and all food made from it. White carbohydrates create insulin spikes that eventually result in insulin and leptin resistance.

In order to avoid any related problems, the type and source of carbohydrates need to be more on the healthier side. Eat as little as possible of sugars (all forms), anything made with fructose, simple starches and all refined foods.

Simple carbohydrates are well known to cause blood sugar and insulin spikes - both contributory factors to obesity and blood sugar problems. Simple carbohydrates have also been found to affect leptin. It follows almost the same pathway as insulin resistance. Upon consumption, simple carbohydrates are rapidly absorbed by the blood, raising the blood sugar levels. In response, the liver secretes a lot of insulin to rapidly bring down high blood sugar. Insulin causes glucose (sugar) in the blood to enter the cells and tissues where they are stored as fats. Up until this point, diabetes can develop if this cycle goes on for some time. With leptin, the process goes further. So, as more fats are produced from the glucose that is being stored, leptin is secreted by these fat cells. Leptin signals the brain to stop eating. However, this signal is overridden by the cravings left by simple carbohydrates. Simple carbohydrates are rapidly digested, absorbed and stored. Hence, it signals the body that it needs to eat more to counter the sudden drop of sugar in the blood. A sort of tug-of-war happens. Increasing leptin levels from increased fat storage signal the body to stop eating. On the other hand, sugar spikes signal the body to eat more. The body has a natural inclination to follow the cravings, as it is deemed more in favor for survival. That is, eating more means more likely to survive, than listening to leptin to curb eating. When this cycle happens often enough, the rest of the body will then start to tune out signals from leptin and resistance develops.

Crash diet and leptin resistance

Repeated crash diets can disrupt the hormonal balance in the body. Leptin is more responsive to states of starvation rather than states of abundance. During restrictive dieting, the body's leptin levels decrease. The decline sends out a hunger signal to the body. In response to the signal, the person is compelled to eat more. Even when the body is already getting the needed nutrition and calorie requirements, the response to stop eating proceeds much slower. Hence, it is easier to eat too much. This is because the body is designed for self-preservation, to continually store up energy for later use to ensure survival.

Cycles of crash diets and overeating cause the body tissues to be less sensitive to leptin. When the body starts to get used to the starvation (during crash dieting) and overeating cycle, it learns to anticipate and prepares well for it. The body learns to tune out hunger suppressing signals from leptin while on binge eating, because it has to prepare for the next starvation cycle. With that, the body slowly accumulates excess weight until it develops obesity.

High Triglycerides

Triglycerides prevent leptin from crossing the blood-brain barrier. If leptin cannot enter the brain, it cannot give the message to curb eating. It is important to watch out for foods that increase the levels of triglycerides on the body. This includes alcohol and sugar. Foods rich in carbohydrates also raise triglycerides levels, such as pasta, rice, bread and potatoes.

Other causes

- Chronic high stress levels

- Overeating

- Eating plenty of simple carbohydrates

- Inadequate sleep

- Chronic high levels of insulin

- Too much exercise, particularly if there is an existing hormonal imbalance

- Consumption of grain and lectin

What are the symptoms of Leptin resistance?

Leptin resistance is often associated with the following symptoms:

- Hunger and cravings for sweet foods and foods rich in refined carbohydrates

- Stress eating

- Urge to eat late at night

- Weight gain, especially around the middle of the body (central obesity)

- Difficulty in getting weight to decrease to desirable goal weight

- High tendency to go on yo-yo dieting

- Symptoms of thyroid imbalance

- Infertility

The body also changes while on leptin resistance. The taste buds are desensitized to sweet foods. This means that the taste buds are less able to sense or taste sweet foods. With this, the body tends to crave more sweets as it does not become satisfied due to lack of sweet sensation on the taste buds. This is often restored once leptin resistance is reversed.

Chapter 3: Leptin and Weight

Leptin is linked to weight regulation. High levels of leptin in the body mean a higher rate of fat burning. Low levels of leptin means fat burning proceeds slower.

Paradoxically, as the body becomes more obese, it also produces less leptin. Fat cells produce leptin but as more fats are synthesized and stored, less leptin is produced and released. This is because leptin levels are more responsive to starvation, rather than to overeating. Simply put, during starvation, the body is more responsive to leptin. That is, starvation lowers leptin levels and the cells easily detect the decrease and reacts to it immediately by increasing food intake. When the body receives more food, leptin levels rise, but the cells are oblivious to the leptin. It tends to "enjoy" the benefits of eating, rather than succumbing to the "anti-eating" leptin signals.

If the body has less carbohydrate and general nutrient intake, leptin levels drop in order to promote more fat storage. If the body keeps hoarding fats, leptin levels react slower and eventually becomes resistant to the few leptin circulating in the blood. The body is essentially more reactive to starvation. Technically, eating more is not threatening the body to be damaged, hence, it does not make much effort to curb eating. To the body, eating more actually helping to stock on energy it may need in some future time.

The presence of leptin resistance makes it more difficult to burn fats and to curb cravings. People who have this condition find themselves always hungry despite recently eating full meals or snacks. They feel hungry sooner and tend to eat more than the average before they feel full. With this, people with leptin resistance tend to have a higher risk for weight gain and obesity.

The main focus of controlling weight in leptin resistance is to control the urge to eat. Certain conditions aggravate overeating and increased cravings in leptin resistance, which include:

- Consumption of HFCS (high fructose corn syrup)

- Eating a lot of simple carbohydrates

- Stress

- Inadequate sleep

To gain more control over hunger and cravings, here are a few guidelines:

- Deal with hunger early in the day.

  Get a good start on controlling huger early in the day. Have a good breakfast with oatmeal. Several studies have shown that oatmeal is one of the best foods to have for breakfast. It is filling and satisfying but does not throw off insulin and leptin levels. Oatmeal gives energy in continuous and steady levels throughout the day. This way, the body does not go into sugar highs and lows that usually prompt cravings and overeating.

Peanut butter is another good food. It is rich in proteins and good fats which provides a steady supply of energy throughout the day.

- Supplements

  Certain supplements help improve the leptin resistance in the body.

- The 12-hour food break

  Give the body a 12-hour break from food. For example, if one had dinner at 9 pm, the next meal should be at breakfast, 9 am the next day. This time span allows the body to use all recently consumed carbohydrates. Recently consumed proteins and fats are also digested and used immediately. This time span also helps to reset the body's hormonal signaling system.

Chapter 4: Reversing Leptin Resistance with Diet

Modifying and controlling the diet is the most important step towards improving leptin resistance. Certain food sources create hormonal imbalance in the body, including leptin imbalance. Numerous studies have shown that the most effective way to reverse leptin resistance is to prevent surges in blood sugar levels. And the best way to do this is through diet management.

Diet Guidelines

Aside from choosing the right foods, it is also important to note a few dietary guidelines to reverse leptin resistance further.

- Avoid severely restricting calorie intake

  Most people think that severely restricting the caloric intake is good for weight loss and health in general. The body runs on calories. If taken in really small amounts, the body recognizes the situation as starvation. Once in the starvation mode, the body kicks into a self-preservation approach. Systems are prepped for nutritive function. Hunger sensation and digestive process are activated. It will also keep fat burning at the bare minimum. Get just enough calories to prevent the body from thinking it is starving.

- Lose weight

  Hormonal imbalance is often closely linked with excess weight. Maintaining ideal weight helps to normalize hormone activity and can reverse leptin resistance.

- Get some carb-day if on a no-carb diet

  Some diets, like raw diet, paleo and Atkins, have very little (if none at all) carbohydrate intake. As was mentioned earlier, this will cause the body to go on starvation mode. Prevent this by designating a "re-feed day". Give the body a boost by consuming 100% to 150% more than the normal daily carbohydrate intake. This will actually jolt the body back into its normal functioning. Resume the chosen diet the next day, after "refeeding" with carbs.

  To further balance the intake on carb cheat or refeed days, consume proteins. Aim to eat 1 gram of protein per 1 pound of body weight. Fat intake should be as low as possible.

- Avoid "yo-yo" diets

  This is most probably the worst diet practice anyone can do. This will mess up the hormonal balance in the body, not to mention the entire homeostatic process. Yo-yo diets often cause a permanent change in the body's functioning. One most often ends up gaining back whatever weight was lost. Worse, most people often gain even more weight than what was lost. Choose weight loss diets well. Choose one that is more sustainable and applicable to lifestyle, needs and health.

- Avoid crash diets

  Crash diets are notoriously known for quick weight loss. However, the effect is pretty much a cross between the starvation mode and the yo-yo diet effect. It will not do anything good with hormonal balance.

Food Choices

Fructose

Limit the fructose. This compound is found in abundance in processed foods. It is also found naturally in fruits- hence the name, fructose or fruit sugar. Experts recommend limiting fructose consumption to 15 to 25 grams in a day for people who suffer from high blood pressure, high cholesterol levels and diabetes. People with normal weight and not suffering from any chronic disease will need to limit fructose consumption as well, though no definite range has yet been established.

Avoid all things processed, as they are likely to be high on HFCS. It is often used as a sweetener in most highly sugary processed foods and snacks such as cookies and sodas. It is also used in some canned fruits and other processed food, as part of the sweetener and as preservative.

Fructose can also be found in fruits as natural fruit sugars. Some fruits have higher amounts of fructose, some lower. It is not recommended to stay away from fruits, as they are also packed with vitamins, phytonutrients and minerals. These compounds have a whole spectrum of health benefits that one can miss out on if not eating fruits. In order to reap the health benefit of fruits and at the same time limit fructose consumption, choose fruits with low fructose levels. Fruits that are low in fructose include berries, lime, kiwi, lemon and grapefruit. Fruit juices, dried fruit, pears and red apples are some of the few that have high fructose content. Even if it is in natural form, it is still fructose and can still affect leptin resistance.

Carbohydrates

Rapidly absorbed simple carbohydrates need to be avoided, too. This includes all food made with white, refined flour such as white bread. Also, avoid anything with refined or white sugar.

Choose the healthier forms of carbohydrates. It can be found in whole, unprocessed foods. Good sources include quinoa, whole oats and pastas made from whole wheat. The general guide when it comes to carbohydrate sources is this- The browner, the better. This means the least processing done, the more intact the nutrients are and the healthier the fruits are.

Proteins

Eating proteins are essential to keep the body healthy and balancing the hormones. Best time to get in a few good proteins is at breakfast.

It is also a good time to get in large amounts of healthy fats and proteins in the morning. Not only is it filling, it also promotes satiety for a long time. Proteins also provide the building blocks for hormone production.

For most people, breakfast cereals constitute a "good breakfast". The truth is, cereals are not a good food idea where leptin is concerned. Cereals contain lectin, a compound that has a particular affinity to leptin. Lectin binds with leptin in the blood, which prevents leptin from binding with cellular receptors. This situation prevents leptin from effectively functioning.

Fats

Fats are not totally bad for the health- as long as they are the healthier types of fats. Choose to get 50% to 70% f fats in the diet. The best ones are monounsaturated and saturated fats. These can be obtained from avocados, coconut, butter, coconut oil and nuts. Some animal fats, too are healthy. Animal-based oil like krill oil and fish oil are rich in beneficial essential fatty acids called omega-3 fatty acid.

Omega-3 Fatty acids

This is one of the healthiest fats anyone can get. In relation to leptin, omega-3 fatty acids increase the tissues' sensitivity to the hormone. Best sources of omega-3 are from fish, like salmon, trout, herring, mackerel and the like. Chia seeds are one of the few good non-animal omega-3 sources.

Omega-3 fatty acids help improve leptin levels and leptin resistance by reducing inflammation in the body. Inflammation reduces the functioning of the cellular leptin receptors. By reducing inflammation, leptin has better chances of carrying and getting its message across. Daily omega-3 fats intake, however, should not exceed 3 grams, as the excess fats can still be a threat to the body.

Avoid foods with high amounts of omega-6 fatty acids. This compound promotes inflammation in the body that can reduce leptin in the body and worsen leptin resistance. Omega-6-rich foods include grains, meats and vegetable oils.

Fruits and Vegetables

Eating fruits and vegetables is one of the great ways to curb hunger while avoiding carbohydrate loading. These are ideal for weight loss in addition to providing many nutrients. These foods send signals to the brain that it is already full but without the consumption of additional calories.

Fiber in fruits and vegetables actually helps address leptin resistance. If leptin's signal to curb overeating is being ignored, fiber steps in. This compound helps in making one feel full earlier into a meal. Good fiber-rich sources include beans, peas, almonds, broccoli, lentils, raspberries and oats, among others. A recommendation is taking 2.5 cups of vegetables and 2 cups of fruits a day to reap the benefits. Note that these foods are better consumed whole and fresh rather in juice form. Juices tend to have more sugar than fibers. The concentrated sugars will not give much help towards improving leptin.

Snacks and sweeteners

Snacks can really disrupt the balance in the body if not eaten in moderation. More than a handful of nuts or a handful of chips can seriously put the sugar and leptin levels out of sync. Snacking can also feed cravings that can seriously derail any weight loss diet.

Recognize that snacking is a way to feed the body's need for quick energy or for perking up. There is nothing with wrong with that. The problem lies on what one snacks on. There is an array of healthy snacks to choose from. To further resist temptation and falling off the wagon, have pre-packaged healthy snacks ready. A handful of mixed nuts in convenient small packages or a small bowl of ready-to-eat vegetable slices can satisfy snacking needs and still be healthy.

Zinc

Studies have shown a close link between obesity, leptin resistance, and zinc deficiency. Incidentally, people who have leptin resistance also have zinc deficiencies and were also generally obese.

Load up on zinc with foods such as nuts, cocoa, mushroom, seafood (particularly oysters), spinach, beans and pumpkin. Beef and lamb, too are rich in zinc.

Specific Foods to Help Reverse Leptin Resistance

Unprocessed oatmeal

This is one of the best foods recommended in reversing leptin resistance and in increasing the body's metabolism. The benefits from eating oatmeal include the following:

- Low GI (glycemic index) carbohydrate that works well with controlling insulin spikes that can also influence leptin resistance

- Packed with fiber that helps in feeling full quicker and longer

- Packed with nutrients, vitamins and minerals that can help in balancing hormones

- Gives power boost with all the nutrients, which makes it a great breakfast item

- Helps lower cholesterol in the blood, which improves leptin responsiveness

Grapefruit

Grapefruit helps in lowering insulin levels that can help reverse leptin resistance. The compounds in grapefruit speed up metabolism, which helps the body to burn more calories, instead of storing them as fat tissues.

Peppers

Capsaicin in hot peppers is great for weight loss. This compound increases the rate of metabolism hours after peppers are consumed. Weight loss helps in improving leptin resistance by improving overall hormonal balance.

Yogurt

Yogurt is loaded with protein and calcium. Protein helps to provide the necessary building blocks in hormone production, specifically leptin. More leptin means better signaling. Calcium is an ion that helps with cellular signaling and transport. Calcium allows certain molecules to enter the cells, which includes hormones like leptin. More calcium means more help for leptin to enter cells and give the message to stop eating.

Both protein and calcium also helps regulate the digestive tract. This helps in dealing with hunger and appetite. A good functioning digestive tract means it is able to process food in a more controlled manner, helping to avoid overeating.

Poultry and Lean Meats

These are meat portions with low fat that provide a good amount of protein. The digestive process requires more energy in order to digest tough proteins. This way, the body burns more calories in digesting proteins. Aside from this, proteins also provide a steady supply of energy, helping in preventing the body from getting hungry early.

Fish

Fish is not only a healthy protein source; it is also rich in healthy fats. Fish oil is abundant in omega3 fatty acids that help improve the body's lipid profile. It also helps to boost the body's metabolism, regulating leptin levels. Omega-3 fats help lower the leptin levels, which helps in reversing leptin resistance. Aim to eat fish like salmon, trout, halibut and mackerel at least twice a week.

Green tea

Besides water, green tea is the next best beverage in terms of health benefits. The caffeine in green tea slightly increases the heart rate. A higher heart rate means faster metabolism. Unlike coffee, green tea can give the caffeine boost but will not affect the insulin levels. Also, the chemical EGCG in green tea stimulates the body's nervous system. This stimulation causes the body to burn more calories in less amount of time.

Broccoli

This cruciferous vegetable is very effective in boosting the metabolism. It is high in calcium and vitamin C. Together, these nutrients stimulates the body to burn calories faster. Faster burning of calories means faster weight loss.

Walnuts and Almonds

Most people will not consider these nuts when trying to lose weight. These are high in calories but contain a good amount of beneficial essential fatty acids. In moderate amounts, these nuts can increase the body's rate of metabolism. Eating a handful of them each day is recommended. These nuts make healthy, protein-rich snacks, which can be filling and satisfying. They can also be added to salads for added crunch and flavor.

Chapter 5: Improving Leptin with Exercise

Leptin resistance is remedied mainly through diet and exercise. Exercise helps hormones function better. It also improves cellular resistance. Exercise stimulates fat burning and better use of fuel and hormones in the body. It keeps the body's gears up and running. The body is like a machine, which needs to be used constantly in order to prevent rusting.

Before exercising, relax and let the body heal first. That is, get adequate sleep and do some stress reduction techniques. Stress and exercise will not be good for the body. Exercising while the body's stress level is high will only worsen the negative stress-induced effects. Stress in any form unbalances the body's hormones.

Perform exercises in the evening so that the full effect will be on the hormone balance. Morning exercises tend to concentrate on giving energy for the body to use for the rest of the day. Evening exercises tend to concentrate more on healing and balancing the body's different systems.

Stress can also stem from the type of exercise, so it is important to choose exercises carefully.

Start with weight lifting and sprints. These induce burst of energy that revs up the metabolism. Walking and swimming are good start-up exercises, too.

High intensity training and weight lifting exercises are good ones to start with. The hormones get a good workout, but without the negative effects of stress.

Avoid cardio exercises. This type of exercise induces stress in the body. It does not do much towards improving leptin resistance.

Other good exercises to improve hormonal balance include walking, stretching, and strength training.

Aerobics

Aerobics is the best choice of exercise to improve leptin function. This is also a great exercise to burn fats. An hour of aerobics can give a good hormonal reset in the body.

Studies have shown that performing aerobic exercises helps in curbing the appetite. This type of exercise increases the levels of BDNF (brain-derived neutrophic factor) in the body. This compound improves brain function by rejuvenating it. BDNF also stimulates the area of the brain that is responsible for suppressing the appetite.

Aside from the BDNF, aerobic exercises also help reverse leptin resistance. This exercise activates more leptin receptors where leptin can bind and do its functions.

Exercising causes sweating. It also stimulates the lymphatic system to move lymph and toxins faster. The collected excess compounds, water and toxins in the lymph are all brought to the sweat glands. When the body sweats during exercise, toxins are released from the body. Therefore, aerobic exercises not only help in weight loss and leptin resistance, it also detoxifies the body. By removing toxins, the cells are cleaned up, making them more responsive to hormonal signaling (i.e., leptin susceptibility).

Chapter 6: Improving Leptin with Lifestyle Changes

In addition to exercise and diet, certain factors also influence and play important roles in the body's homeostatic processes. They may seem trivial and unrelated to the leptin problem, but they can help regulate the levels of this hormone. Leptin resistance is resolved better and faster when a holistic approach is used.

<u>Sleep</u>

Optimize sleep. Numerous studies have shown that sleep has a profound effect on the body's hormonal system. It is during sleep that the body resets its signaling systems. Also, the body heals and repairs itself during sleep. The body tends to provide energy and give more attention to muscle activity during active hours. Repair and adjustment in other homeostatic systems takes a back seat in favor of fueling muscle activity when awake. It only gets to rest and heal during sleep.

Inadequate sleep means inadequate opportunity for rest, healing and readjustment. Studies have shown that leptin levels drop by as much as 15 percent in people who do not get adequate sleep. Aim to sleep at least 7 hours at night.

Notice that when there is inadequate sleep, one wakes up tired and hungry. The body also craves for high carbohydrate foods in an attempt to provide more energy for the day's activities. All throughout the day, the body does not recover from the hunger. A person continues to eat but hunger seems to be persistent. This is because leptin balance is thrown off when there is inadequate sleep.

Do not eat or snack at least four hours before going to bed. Otherwise, the body will concentrate on digesting and storing the recently consumed food during sleep instead of repairing and healing the body.

Avoid all forms of snacks and caloric drinks such as fruit and vegetable juices. Water is OK to drink before bedtime. However, do so in moderation. Nighttime urination can disrupt sleep. Also, coffee and teas are OK but omit the cream and sugar. These drinks do have some level of caffeine so drink only a little. Caffeine can disrupt sleep.

Also, sleep can actually help in burning fat and losing weight. As has been mentioned previously, weight loss helps in reversing leptin resistance. During sleep, fat burning is at its peak. Thus, getting at least 7 hours of sleep means burning fats for at least 7 hours without having to sweat it out in the gym.

<u>Stress reduction</u>

Stress alone can easily put every bodily process out of sync. In leptin resistance, stress is a threat to self-preservation. Thus, it can actually promote more eating and fat storage, worsening leptin resistance.

Lowering the level of stress allows the body to feel that it is no longer threatened, so no need to keep eating and hoarding fats. Relaxing the body also helps to reboot the system, helping in reversing leptin resistance.

Chapter 7: Leptin Supplements

Supplementation can also help in improving leptin resistance. Studies have shown that taking certain supplements help in improving weight. It also helps regulate the leptin levels in the body.

It is considered as a good remedy for people who feel lethargic from lack of sleep. Leptin supplements temporarily get the leptin levels back on track, which has been otherwise thrown off balance by inadequate sleep.

A person should be aware that commercially prepared leptin supplements do not necessarily contain the hormone leptin. Most supplements do not even have any trace of the hormone in its pills and powders. These supplements most likely have compounds that stimulate the body to produce more leptin or be more responsive to leptin.

How Leptin Supplements Work

Leptin supplements work in three ways: improving cellular response to leptin, increasing the production of leptin, or increasing the levels by adding extrinsic (made outside of the body) leptin to the body.

Some supplements contain compounds that stimulate the fat cells to produce more leptin. It also helps reverse leptin resistance by stimulating other tissues in the body to produce leptin in higher amounts in order to improve leptin levels.

Leptin supplements can work by influencing the brain. It stimulates brain areas to stimulate reserve fat tissues to release leptin. The body normally has fat reserves, which acts as an emergency supply in case of starvation. Weight gain interferes with the normal balance between fat reserves and leptin release. As more fats are added and converted as fat reserves, the more difficult these reserves become at releasing leptin. In the presence of leptin supplements, the brain is stimulated to release certain compounds that demand these fat reserves to release leptin. This way, leptin levels are improved.

Some supplements, although very few, have very small amounts of leptin. These supplements work by providing an extrinsic source of leptin. That is, taking these supplements is taking in more leptin produced from outside the body. These supplements are very rare, as any supplement that contains hormones are subjected to FDA regulations. They are often considered more as drugs because of the synthetic hormones they contain, rather than as mere supplements.

Irvingia supplement

This supplement is obtained from the extract of an African mango. Studies have shown that Irvingia supplement helps improve weight and fat distribution. Hip and waist circumference improves with this supplement. Better fat distribution and regulation improves leptin levels and resistance.

Adults are advised to take 150 milligrams of Irvingia supplement two times a day. It should be taken with food to improve absorption of the active compounds. If side effects such as nausea, headache, bloating, gassiness and sleeplessness occur, stop taking Irvingia supplements. Also, pregnant and breastfeeding mothers are not advised to take this supplement due to potential risks.

Chapter 8: Natural Ways to Boost Leptin

There are also some natural ways that can help reverse leptin resistance and improve leptin levels. These may not have the profound effects that diet and exercise give, but these would still help.

Mindfulness

This is a holistic way of reversing leptin resistance by breaking the overfeeding cycle. Mindful eating is considered a meditation form which helps the body to control eating patterns that have gone uncontrolled. This is also associated with better weight management, sugar control and feeding behavior.

To do mindfulness eating, one has to concentrate on what foods to eat. That involves telling and conditioning the mind to eat what is healthy and in the right amounts. Deep breathing exercises before, during, and after a meal help in sending a message to the brain and the rest of the body that it is already full. Deep breathing and concentrating on feeling full also helps in curbing the need to sugary foods.

Nutraceuticals

This is about taking certain foods in order to reverse leptin resistance. Nutraceuticals simply means taking food as medicine, or taking advantage of the different natural compounds to heal the body. The following foods have been shown to provide positive benefits on leptin:

Cucurmin

This is a compound found in the spice turmeric. This has been shown in studies to down regulate leptin in the body.

Omega-3 fatty acids

This compound helps in regulating leptin in several ways which includes reducing inflammation that worsen leptin resistance. This compound is found in nuts, seeds and fish.

Probiotics

Probiotics are active microorganisms that help in restoring digestive health and immune balance. By improving digestion, food is better metabolized and sent to the blood. Toxins are also better moved out of the body. Removing toxins can clear the cells of residue that can impede normal metabolic and hormonal responses. Aside from these, probiotics also improve the rate of production of short chain fatty acids by the body. These fatty acids help in better hormonal production and utilization.

Other compounds have also been shown to provide positive feedbacks in reversing leptin resistance, such as the following:

- L-glutamine

- Aloe vera leaf extract

- Vitamin D

- Licorice extract

- Ginger

- Hops

- Rosemary

- Monolaurin

- Garlic

- Green tea extract

Conclusion

Thank you again for downloading this book!

I hope this book was able to help you understand what leptin is all about. It is a hormone that plays a very important role in the body. It needs to be kept in balance in order to have a healthy body. Leptin resistance can cause obesity that increases the risk for a whole lot of different health conditions like diabetes and heart problems. The god news is that there are also several ways to improve leptin function and response in the body.

The next step is to start eating the right foods, exercising the right way and getting enough sleep. Leptin levels can be improved and cellular response can also be enhanced just by making a few small changes. Substituting healthier foods and getting active more often are small, simple tasks that do a whole lot for ensuring hormone balance. Also, start telling others about how to take care of their bodies better. Spread the word about leptin and what it does in the body.

Finally, if you enjoyed this book, please take the time to share your thoughts and post a review on Amazon. It'd be greatly appreciated!

Thank you and good luck!

Printed in Great Britain
by Amazon